2006

 W9-BOO-979

WITHDRAWN

Let Freedom Ring

The Lewis and Clark Expedition

by Susan Bursell

Consultant:
Bob Moore
Jefferson National Expansion Memorial
St. Louis, Missouri

Bridgestone Books
an imprint of Capstone Press
Mankato, Minnesota

Bridgestone Books are published by Capstone Press
151 Good Counsel Drive • P.O. Box 669 • Mankato, Minnesota 56002
www.capstonepress.com

Printed in the United States of America

Library of Congress Cataloging-in-Publication Data
Bursell, Susan, 1951–
    The Lewis and Clark Expedition / by Susan Bursell.
    p. cm. — (Let freedom ring)
    Includes bibliographical references and index.
    Summary: Describes the travels of Meriwether Lewis and William Clark and their Corps
of Discovery and its importance in relation to American Indian tribes and the westward
expansion of the United States.
    ISBN 0-7368-1099-4
    1. Lewis and Clark Expedition (1804–1806)—Juvenile literature. 2. West (U.S.)—
Discovery and exploration—Juvenile literature. 3. West (U.S.)—Description and travel—
Juvenile literature. [1. Lewis and Clark Expedition (1804–1806). 2. West (U.S.)—Discovery
and exploration. 3. Lewis, Meriwether, 1774–1809. 4. Clark, William, 1770–1838. 5.
Sacagawea, 1786–1884. 6. Explorers.] I. Title. II. Series.
F592.7 .B98 2002
917.804′2—dc21   2001005826

Editorial Credits

Rebecca Aldridge and Charles Pederson, editors; Kia Bielke, cover designer, interior
illustrator, and interior layout designer; Jennifer Schonborn, cover production designer and
interior illustrator; Deirdre Barton, photo researcher

Photo Credits

Cover: Courtesy Frederic Remington Art Museum, Ogdensburg, New York (middle),
Stockbyte (bottom left), Nicholas King/Library of Congress (bottom right); Stockbyte, 4, 12,
20, 30, 36; North Wind Picture Archives, 5, 11 (right), 19, 37; Hulton/Archive Photos, 6, 29,
38, 43; National Portrait Gallery, Smithsonian Institution/Art Resource, NY, 9; Capstone
Press/Charles Willson Peale/Independence NHP, 11 (left), 42; CORBIS, 13, 31; National
Museum of American Art, Washington, DC/Art Resource, NY, 17; Unicorn Stock
Photos/Terry Barner, 21; Stock Montage, Inc., 23, 25; David Muench/CORBIS, 27;
Stephen A. Stromstad, 32 (both); AFP/CORBIS, 40

2   3   4   5   6   07   06   05   04   03

Table of Contents

Chapter One

The Dream of Discovery

In 1953, in an attic in St. Paul, Minnesota, a package was found in a desk that had belonged to a general of the U.S. Civil War (1861–1865). The package was wrapped in a newspaper dated 1805. Inside were handwritten notes on scraps of paper. They were field notes from explorer William Clark.

In 1803, Thomas Jefferson had given Clark and Meriwether Lewis specific instructions. Both men were to keep detailed journals of their trip to find the best route from the Missouri River to the Pacific Ocean. Together, the journals tell the story of the Lewis and Clark expedition.

The United States in 1801

In 1801, the Mississippi River marked the western border of the United States. Beyond the U.S. boundaries lay land that Britain, France, Russia, and Spain claimed. These countries wanted as much North American land as

William Clark made the above drawing of a bird in his expedition diary. One historian called Lewis and Clark and their men "the writingest explorers of their time."

possible. Although fur traders from these countries had done some exploring, no one knew much about the area between the Missouri River and the Pacific.

For years, many people thought there must be a Northwest Passage, a waterway across North America to the Pacific Ocean. The nation that charted this route would have a strong claim to the land and its treasures. Thomas Jefferson, who had become U.S. president in 1801, dreamed of finding the Northwest Passage and extending U.S. borders to the Pacific.

The purchase of the Louisiana Territory (shown in the map) doubled the size of the United States.

An Important Purchase

In 1802, Jefferson wanted to buy the port of New Orleans. The French ruler, Napoleon Bonaparte, offered to sell New Orleans and all of the Louisiana Territory. Jefferson's representatives in Paris enthusiastically agreed. Napoleon asked $15 million for about 820,000 square miles (2,123,800 square kilometers) of land. The agreement for the purchase became official April 30, 1803.

Four times, Jefferson tried unsuccessfully to organize an expedition through the West. In January 1803, before the Louisiana Purchase had been made, Jefferson secretly asked Congress to finance an expedition to learn about "the river Missouri, & the Indians inhabiting it." Congress approved the plan in February. Jefferson wanted Meriwether Lewis to lead this "Corps of Discovery."

Meriwether Lewis

Meriwether Lewis was born August 18, 1774, a short distance from Thomas Jefferson's home in Virginia. The men's families were longtime friends.

Lewis was educated in Virginia and was trained to run his family's lands. At age 20, he

Jefferson's Instructions

"The object of your mission is to explore the Missouri river, & such principal stream[s] of it, as, by it's course and communication with the waters of the Pacific Ocean . . . may offer the most direct & practicable water communication across this continent for the purposes of commerce [selling goods for money]."
—Thomas Jefferson to Meriwether Lewis, June 20, 1803

joined the army, serving on the frontier, or edge of settled areas, in Ohio and Pennsylvania. He was promoted to captain at age 28.

In 1801, President Jefferson asked Lewis to be his personal secretary in Washington, D.C. The men discussed Jefferson's plans for exploring the West and his hopes for U.S. expansion. Jefferson also talked about his thirst for scientific knowledge.

Planning the Expedition

In the spring of 1803, Lewis began to plan for the expedition. His main assignment was to find the Northwest Passage and make a map of its route. Jefferson also wanted information about the

American Indians in the West. Jefferson wanted Lewis to learn about their cultures, languages, and relations with other tribes. Lewis was to describe the area's climate, soil, minerals, and fossils. He was to make notes about all the animals and plants he found, collecting samples for science.

Lewis had to buy supplies for a trip that could last two years. To start, he bought 15 of the latest

In the spring of 1803, Lewis visited Philadelphia, Pennsylvania, the center of American science, to prepare for the trip. He learned botany, or the study of plants, and anatomy, or the study of bodies. For several weeks, Lewis also studied medicine and navigation, or how to sail a ship.

rifles, along with axes and knives for hunting and defense. The corps needed navigation instruments, medical supplies, cooking utensils, tools, and presents for the American Indians. The group needed food, clothing, gunpowder, ink, and paper. And of course, they needed boats. Lewis bought a large dog named Seaman to accompany him. Congress had allowed $2,500. Lewis spent almost $40,000.

Choosing Expedition Members

Lewis asked William Clark, one of his commanding officers in the army, to help him lead the expedition. Clark, four years older than Lewis, was born on August 1, 1770. Clark grew up on the Kentucky and Ohio frontier and had fought American Indians. The tall, red-haired man had little formal education but plenty of practical experience in the wild.

Lewis wanted companions with different skills such as hunting, interpreting languages, scouting, or boating. Most were volunteers from the army, but a few civilians came along. Clark brought his childhood companion and slave, York.

By the end of August, a boat was ready. It was 55 feet (16.76 meters) long with 20 oars and a mast that could support a sail. It would carry most of the expedition's supplies. The group also had two smaller boats, called pirogues, that each held at least eight or nine men.

After loading the boats, Lewis set off for St. Louis, Missouri. On the way, the crew picked up Clark, York, and others. In St. Louis, Lewis gathered final supplies and information about the route ahead. Clark trained the men and oversaw the packing and loading of supplies. The Corps of Discovery was almost ready.

William Clark (left) accepted Lewis's offer (above) to join the expedition.

Chapter Two

Up the Wide Missouri

The corps set out on May 14, 1804. The group found the Missouri River to be a challenge. Moving upstream, the men rowed, pushed the boats with poles, or pulled them with ropes. The corps sailed if there was wind. They steered around logs and got stuck on sandbars. The men worked 12 to 14 hours a day.

The river was not the only problem. Rain, wind, and hail slowed the corps. Mosquitoes swarmed so thickly that the men breathed them in. On their skin, the men smeared grease from bears. That helped, as did sleeping under nets at night. But even Seaman howled, complaining about the insects.

New Experiences

The high hills and bluffs of the Missouri opened up to the Great Plains, a rolling grassland with bright wildflowers. The men saw many unfamiliar animals, such as coyotes and jackrabbits. The men skinned and stuffed a

This photo shows the Missouri River as it looks today. Clark wrote that the men worked so hard on the difficult river that sweat ran off them in streams.

badger and an antelope to send back to Jefferson. They preserved red fox skins and rabbit skeletons.

The men spent a whole day trying to catch "barking squirrels," as Lewis called them. Another man named the animals prairie dogs. The men tried to dig one from its hole, then they flushed it out with buckets of water carried from the river. They sent the animal alive for Jefferson to study.

The First Tribes

The expedition was supposed to establish friendly relations with American Indians. These people were

Huge herds of buffalo became a common sight as the corps traveled through the West.

The Only Death

At the end of July 1804, Sergeant Charles Floyd developed a terrible stomachache that probably was appendicitis. He died on August 20 and was buried high on a hill the corps called Floyd's Bluff. Though everyone was sick at some time during the trip, Floyd was the only member who died. Today, Sergeant Floyd's grave can be seen in Sioux City, Iowa.

hard to find because most were hunting buffalo during the summer. In August, the corps met a tribal group and invited them to meet at a place called Council Bluffs.

The corps had a routine for its tribal meetings. The men wore their uniforms and displayed their equipment. Lewis told the tribes that the land belonged to the United States and their "great chief," Jefferson. He explained that Americans wanted peaceful trade and invited the chiefs to visit Washington, D.C. The corps handed out gifts such as face paint, gunpowder, whiskey, and medals picturing Jefferson.

Daily Routine

Each day started with a cold breakfast of leftovers. The men loaded the boats and pushed off. Some men hunted for animal meat. Usually, Lewis walked with Seaman, collecting plants and soil and making notes. Clark drew maps on the boat.

At midday, the men set up camp and gathered wood for lunch, which they called dinner. It was the day's only hot meal. They cooked meat the men had hunted. If there was no fresh meat, they ate a meal of corn and grease, or pork and flour. They also had a small glass of whiskey.

Supper was leftovers again and any wild fruit the men found. They washed down their meal with river water. Clark wrote that every cup of water was half mud. After supper, one of the men might play some music. The group wrote in their journals by firelight. The men took turns guarding the boats and the camp.

When the corps reached Sioux territory at the end of August, the Yankton Sioux greeted them warmly. The Americans raised a U.S. flag, gave speeches, and handed out gifts. Clark made careful notes about the Sioux language and customs.

In September, the explorers met the powerful Teton Sioux. Lewis and Clark held a council, but the Teton language was difficult. The chiefs were disappointed with their gifts and saw the white men as a threat to Teton trading. Three warriors tried to take over one of the pirogues. Clark drew his sword, and the men loaded the cannon on the boat. Warriors readied their bows and arrows. Finally, the Tetons backed down.

Among colorful tepees, the men of the corps enjoyed a feast of dog with the Yankton Sioux, such as the feast shown here.

The Arikara

In early October, the Arikara people welcomed the men near three small villages. York fascinated the Arikara, who had never seen an African American person before. They saw special spiritual power in York's skin color.

A Place to Stay

The weather got colder as the corps moved farther west, and the men looked for Mandan villages. The Mandans and Hidatsas were successful farmers. They lived near each other in five villages totaling about 4,500 people. This was more than the number of people living in St. Louis or Washington, D.C. in 1804.

In November, Lewis and Clark hired interpreters who could speak more than one language. One interpreter was French Canadian trader Toussaint Charbonneau, who spoke French and Hidatsa. He brought along his pregnant young Shoshone wife, Sacagawea. The Hidatsa had captured her about four years earlier. She spoke Hidatsa and Shoshone.

The winter of 1804–1805 was cold. River ice froze so solid that it supported herds of buffalo. The men stayed inside because of the below-freezing temperatures. To prepare for spring, they worked hard building canoes and repairing equipment and clothes. The men of the corps celebrated Christmas by themselves but spent New Year's Day in the villages, sharing food, music, and presents with the tribes.

This photo shows a re-creation of Fort Mandan. The Mandans and Hidatsas helped the corps find the spot for this winter camp.

Chapter Three

West to the Pacific

By April 7, 1805, the river ice had melted, so the large boat returned east with items for Jefferson. The 33-member expedition continued west that same day in the two pirogues and six dugout canoes. The American Indians tried to prepare the explorers for the steep mountains and waterfalls ahead.

River travel still was difficult, and strong winds slowed the corps. The blowing sand was so bad "we [must] eat, drink and breathe it." The men had to walk through icy water or over cactus plants on shore to pull the boat. The ropes they used were rotting.

All the important scientific instruments, medicine, trade goods, and journals were packed in one of the pirogues. One April day, a sudden burst of wind tipped the pirogue and its cargo. Sacagawea held her baby son in one arm and rescued the supplies with her free arm.

Along the river, wildlife was plentiful and unafraid of the

These actors stand on a re-creation of the large boat that returned
east carrying items for Jefferson.

Sacagawea's Son

On February 11, 1805, Sacagawea delivered her baby, Jean Baptiste. Clark called him "Pompy."

corps. The hunters easily supplied their favorite meats of beaver tails and buffalo. Even Seaman hunted. Sacagawea added prairie plants to the meat the group ate.

Decision

On June 3, the corps came to a fork in the Missouri River. Lewis and Clark chose the south fork, hoping to find the Great Falls of the Missouri River, in modern Montana. They knew that the falls would tell the group they were on the right track to the Pacific. The other men disagreed with the choice, but Lewis wrote they were "ready to follow us any where . . ."

On June 13, Lewis heard a muffled roar and saw mist rising in the distance. It was the Great Falls. They had chosen the correct fork. But they would have to portage, or carry, all their boats and supplies 18 miles (29 kilometers) around the falls.

The Mighty Grizzly Bear

In April and May 1805, the corps had its first encounters with grizzly bears. The group learned that sometimes 10 shots were needed to kill a bear. Wounded bears chased the men into the river and across the prairies. One of the expedition members drew the picture below, which shows a bear chasing a group member up a tree.

Lewis figured that one bear the men shot weighed 600 pounds (272 kilograms). Another grizzly had claws that were 7 inches (17.8 centimeters) long and paws 9 inches (22.9 centimeters) across. An excellent watchdog, Seaman often barked at night to warn the group about bears.

Page 239.

An American having struck a Bear but not kill'd him escapes into a Tree.

The month-long portage was difficult. Violent hailstorms bruised and cut the group. Grizzlies and rattlesnakes threatened, yet Lewis thought the worst hardships were gnats, mosquitoes, and cactuses. The corps needed new moccasins every few days. Sacagawea became ill with a high fever. Lewis convinced her to drink water from a nearby sulfur spring, and she gradually recovered.

On the Missouri Again

On July 15, 1805, the expedition was back on the Missouri River. The group crossed steep, wooded canyons that Lewis called the "Gates of the Rocky Mountains." Sacagawea recognized the area called Three Forks, where she had been kidnapped years earlier. This was Shoshone Indian territory.

On August 12, Lewis and three of his men found the source of the Missouri River. Lewis also climbed the Continental Divide. In this place in the Rockies, rivers on one side flow east, and the rivers on the other side flow west. From the divide, Lewis hoped to see grasslands leading to the Columbia River. Instead, he saw "high mountains still to the West." He saw that there was no Northwest Passage.

The next day, Lewis and his men saw three Shoshone women, who led them to the tribe's camp. At a council with the Shoshone, Sacagawea and Charbonneau were translating. Suddenly, Sacagawea stopped and stared at Chief Cameahwait. Crying, she jumped up and hugged him. Cameahwait was her brother.

Lewis (on rock) catches his first sight of the Rocky Mountains.

The corps named the spot Camp Fortunate because of their good luck there. The corps got the horses needed to carry supplies across the mountains before winter began. A Shoshone guide agreed to lead them over the mountains.

Across the Mountains

In late August, the corps was ready for a difficult part of the trip into the Bitterroot Mountains. Snow, sleet, and rain fell as the group climbed steep mountain paths. In early September, the corps camped at a spot they called Travelers Rest to prepare to cross the snowy mountains.

On September 11, 1805, the corps began the worst part of the trail. Several horses slipped and fell off the narrow, snowy path. The group was running out of food. Meat was so scarce, the men killed and ate three horses. By the 18th, the men were weak from hunger.

After 11 days, the group left the Bitterroot Mountains. They entered a valley where they found the Nez Percé. This tribe shared salmon and plant roots with the starved men. The tribe showed them how to make canoes by using fire to hollow out pine trees. The men branded their horses and left them with the tribe.

The corps loaded five new dugouts and pushed them into the Clearwater River on October 7. The men had left the United States and entered Oregon Territory.

The Clearwater led to the Snake River, and then to the Columbia. Going downstream, the corps made 20 to 30 miles (32 to 48 kilometers) a day. The rapid current often tipped over the dugouts as the corps hurried to reach the Pacific before winter came.

This image shows Lost Trail Pass, the path the expedition took through the Bitterroot Mountains.

Sacagawea

Sacagawea helped the Corps of Discovery in many ways. Clark realized that a woman's presence showed the party's peaceful intentions, "as no woman ever accompanies a war party of Indians in this quarter." Sacagawea knew which wild plants were safe to eat. Lewis wrote that as an interpreter, Sacagawea was the group's only hope for friendly relations with the Shoshone, "on whom we depend for horses to assist us in our portage from the Missouri to the Columbia river." Clark thought highly of Sacagawea: "[She deserved] a greater reward for her attention and services . . . than we had in our power to give her."

In 2000, the United States produced a new dollar coin. On the front is an image of Sacagawea carrying her infant son, Jean Baptiste. Her image was chosen for the coin to honor her "role as an American woman pioneer."

Native peoples lined the banks to watch the corps run the rapids. Sometimes, tribesmen helped the group carry canoes and supplies past the worst stretches. These American Indians wore clothes made from cedar bark or jackets they had received from European sailors. The jackets proved that the

Pacific Ocean was near. The corps envied the carved canoes of these American Indians, which tipped less easily than dugouts.

On November 7, 1805, Clark wrote in his journal: "Ocian [Ocean] in View! O! the joy." But what the corps thought was the ocean was really Gray's Bay. The group actually reached the ocean on November 14. Clark estimated they were 4,162 miles (6,698 kilometers) from their starting point at the mouth of the Missouri. His estimation was off by only about 40 miles (64 kilometers).

Sacagawea's name means Bird Woman in the Hidatsa language. Legend says she guided the corps to the ocean, though she really helped them only when she saw familiar landmarks near where she grew up. The statue at right honors her.

Chapter Four

Longing for Home

Finding a winter campsite was the next order of business for the corps. After listening to advice from the Chinook and Clatsop Indians, the corps chose a place on the Columbia River where there was good elk hunting for food and clothing.

That winter at Fort Clatsop had only 12 days without rain. The damp air spoiled food and rotted clothes. Fleas were everywhere.

The corps members kept busy. They preserved meat, sewed clothes and 338 pairs of moccasins, and made salt from seawater. Clark worked on small maps of places they explored and a large map of their whole route. Lewis wrote about local tribes, as well as animals and plants new to science.

The Clatsops and Chinooks visited regularly but were not as welcoming as the Mandans and Hidatsas had been. The Clatsops and Chinooks wanted high prices for the items they sold, and they took things from the men. But their canoes were better than any

The Chinook people lived in lodges like the one shown here.

the corps had seen, and the tribes made waterproof hats and baskets.

On Their Way

In the spring, the corps became eager to start for home. They paddled up the Columbia River on March 23, 1806. By early May, the expedition reached the Nez Percé to gather the horses left in the tribe's care.

When mountain snow finally melted, the corps traveled quickly to Travelers Rest, where it

On July 25, Clark's group found an unusual sandstone formation in what is now Montana. Clark named it Pompy's Tower. Clark carved the date and his name on the rock. His name is still there today.

An Embarrassing Wound

A day before rejoining Clark's group, Lewis and another corps member were hunting. The man, who had poor eyesight, mistook Lewis for an elk and shot him in the buttocks. The painful wound was not dangerous but took several weeks to heal.

split into two groups. Clark's group explored the Yellowstone River to the south. Lewis and a smaller group traveled up the Marias River to its source. The two groups planned to meet in a month where the Yellowstone and Missouri Rivers joined.

Clark's group reached Three Forks, where they found canoes and supplies they had stored. Several men paddled to the Great Falls. The rest went overland by horseback to the Yellowstone.

At the Great Falls, Lewis's group found their hidden supplies and specimens. Lewis and three men explored the Marias. Returning across the territory of the fierce Blackfeet people, Lewis's group met eight men of that tribe. Cautiously, the groups agreed to talk and camp together that night.

Near dawn, the Blackfeet tried to steal the corps' rifles and horses. In the struggle, one Blackfeet man was stabbed and another shot. The rest rode off. To escape the tribe's revenge, Lewis and his men rode 120 miles (193 kilometers) in 24 hours to reach the Missouri River.

Cheers in St. Louis

Lewis and Clark met at the Yellowstone River on August 12, 1806. From there, they continued to the Mandan villages. The corps left the Mandans in mid-August. Charbonneau, Sacagawea, and Pompy stayed behind. Clark paid Charbonneau $500.33 for his services. One tribal chief accompanied the corps to meet President Jefferson.

Along the river, the corps surprised some traders. It had been so long since hearing from the Corps of Discovery that most people in the eastern United States believed they had died.

On September 23, 1806, the men raised a happy shout when St. Louis came into sight. The townspeople lined the banks and cheered. The Corps of Discovery had traveled more than 8,000 miles (12,900 kilometers) in two and a half years.

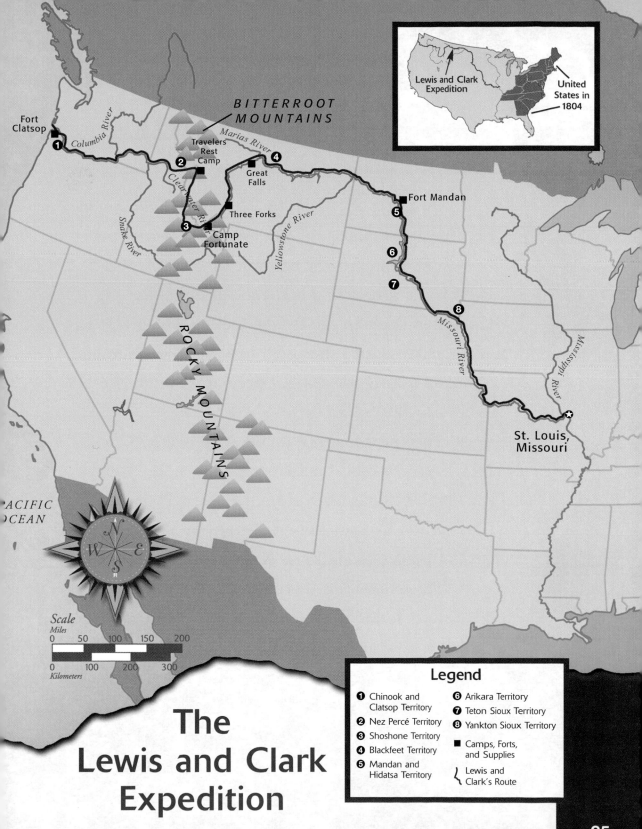

BITTERROOT
MOUNTAINS

Marias River

Travelers
Rest
Camp

Great
Falls

Three Forks

Camp
Fortunate

Columbia River

Fort
Clatsop

Clearwater River

Snake River

Yellowstone River

Fort Mandan

Missouri River

Mississippi River

ROCKY MOUNTAINS

PACIFIC
OCEAN

St. Louis,
Missouri

**Lewis and Clark
Expedition**

**United
States in
1804**

Scale
Miles
0   50   100   150   200

0   100   200   300
Kilometers

The
Lewis and Clark
Expedition

Legend

1 Chinook and
   Clatsop Territory

2 Nez Percé Territory

3 Shoshone Territory

4 Blackfeet Territory

5 Mandan and
   Hidatsa Territory

6 Arikara Territory

7 Teton Sioux Territory

8 Yankton Sioux Territory

■ Camps, Forts,
   and Supplies

∿ Lewis and
   Clark's Route

Chapter Five

Home Again

On December 2, 1806, President Jefferson gave his annual message to Congress. He reported that the Corps of Discovery had traced the Missouri River to its source and had canoed down the Columbia River to the Pacific Ocean. The group had accurately mapped the geography of their route and obtained information about previously unknown American Indian tribes.

The corps had not found an all-water Northwest Passage, because there was none. But as the first U.S. citizens to cross the Great Plains, the Continental Divide, and the Bitterroot Mountains, the corps staked a claim in the West for the United States.

The expedition was successful in other ways. The group found and described 178 plants and 122 animals new to science. The corps carefully preserved samples to bring back for others to study. The corps met more than 40 American Indian tribes. Clark's map

Prickly pear cactus was one of the many plants that Lewis and Clark encountered and wrote about during their expedition.

was the first to correctly illustrate the continent. His map showed the way for future traders, trappers, explorers, and settlers. The corps' method of scientific observation and recording information became a model for others.

Afterward

After returning to the United States, Lewis was appointed governor of the Louisiana Territory. But he had financial, political, and health problems. In

This map of some of the area covered during the Lewis and Clark expedition was drawn by expedition member Robert Frazier.

Some Expedition Discoveries

The corps did not really discover the plants and animals below. American Indians had known about them for hundreds of years. But Lewis and Clark were the first to write about them for science.

Plants	Animals	
Orange honeysuckle	American bison	Lewis's Woodpecker
Osage orange	Bighorn sheep	Mountain goat
Sagebrush	Coyote	Prairie dog
Wild licorice	Grizzly bear	Pronghorn antelope
	Jackrabbit	

October 1809, Lewis traveled to Washington, D.C., to straighten out his finances. He stopped at an inn and apparently shot himself to death.

Clark became Superintendent of Indian Affairs and governor of the Missouri Territory. He named his first son Meriwether Lewis Clark. Called the "Red-Headed Chief" by the tribes, Clark worked hard to protect them until his death in 1838.

Sacagawea and Charbonneau continued to live with tribes on the Missouri River, interpreting and

Expedition Honors

On January 17, 2001, President Bill Clinton (below right) awarded Sacagawea and York the title of honorary sergeants in the army. Rose Anne Abrahamson (left), a descendant of Cameahwait, of the Lemhi Shoshone Tribe, and Amy Mossett (center) of the Mandan-Hidatsa-Arikara Nation accepted the honor.

Clinton promoted Clark to the rank of captain in the U.S. Army, the same rank Lewis had held. At the time of the expedition, Clark was officially a second lieutenant.

trapping. In 1812, Sacagawea had a daughter named Lisette. Sacagawea died that winter.

Jean Baptiste Charbonneau, "Pompy," along with Lisette, lived with Clark as a child. He was educated in St. Louis and studied in Europe for five years. He returned to the United States and worked as a fur trapper, guide, judge, and interpreter for explorers and soldiers. He died in 1866.

When York returned from the expedition, he asked Clark for his freedom. About 10 years after the expedition, Clark finally freed York and helped him set up a freight business. York died in 1832.

White traders and settlers gradually moved west and took over American Indian land. They brought disease, foreign customs, and war, which forever changed the American Indian way of life.

By the time the last expedition member died in 1870, the United States included 37 states. Jefferson had estimated it would take hundreds of years to settle the continent, but it was done in less than one hundred.

TIMELINE

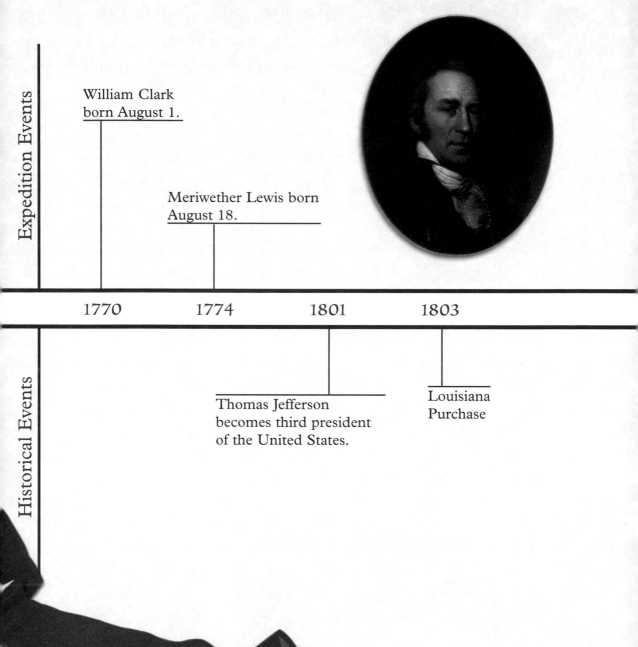

Expedition Events

William Clark born August 1.

Meriwether Lewis born August 18.

1770   1774   1801   1803

Historical Events

Thomas Jefferson becomes third president of the United States.

Louisiana Purchase

May 14: The Corps of Discovery leaves winter camp for the West.

August: First councils with American Indian tribes

August 20: Sergeant Floyd dies.

September–October: Council with Teton Sioux, Arikara, Mandans, and Hidatsas

November: Charbonneau and Sacagawea join the corps.

Winter: Fort Mandan

June–July: Great Falls, camp and portage

August 12: Climb Continental Divide

September: Meet Nez Percé

October: Reach Columbia River

Winter: Fort Clatsop

March 23: Leave for the East

September 23: Reach St. Louis

1804   1805   1806

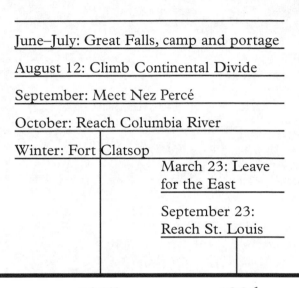

Glossary

anatomy (uh-NAT-uh-mee)—the study of the structure of animal bodies

appendicitis (uh-pen-duh-SYE-tiss)—a condition in which the small, closed tube leading from the large intestine becomes painful

botany (BOT-uh-nee)—the study of plant life

Continental Divide (kon-tuh-NENT-uhl duh-VIDE)—the highest point of North America dividing waters flowing west from those flowing east

corps (KOR)—a military unit working together under direction

frontier (fruhn-TIHR)—a region that borders settled territory

interpreter (in-TUR-prit-ur)—a person who converts one language into another

journal (JUR-nuhl)—a written record of experiences and events

Northwest Passage (north-WEST PASS-ij)—a nonexistent path by water between the Atlantic and Pacific Oceans in North America

portage (PORT-ij)—to carry boats and gear overland from one body of water to another or around waterfalls and other obstacles

specimen (SPESS-uh-muhn)—an item typical of a group, which is used for study

For Further Reading

Anderson, Dale. *Westward Expansion.* Making of America. Austin, Tex.: Raintree Steck-Vaughn, 2001.

Edwards, Judith. *Lewis and Clark's Journey of Discovery in American History.* In American History. Springfield, N.J.: Enslow Publishers, 1999.

Gunderson, Mary. *Cooking on the Lewis and Clark Expedition.* Exploring History through Simple Recipes. Mankato, Minn.: Blue Earth Books, 2000.

Karwoski, Gail Langer. *Seaman: The Dog Who Explored the West with Lewis & Clark.* Atlanta: Peachtree, 1999.

Kozar, Richard. *Lewis and Clark.* Philadelphia: Chelsea House Publishers, 2000.

Schanzer, Rosalyn. *How We Crossed the West: The Adventures of Lewis & Clark.* Washington, D.C.: National Geographic Society, 1997.

Van Steenwyk, Elizabeth. *My Name Is York.* Flagstaff, Ariz.: Rising Moon/Books for Young Readers from Northland Publishing Company, 1997.

Places of Interest

Fort Abraham Lincoln State Park
4480 Fort Lincoln Road
Mandan, ND 58554
http://www.ndparks.com/parks/flsp.htm
Historic fort that includes earth lodges like those of the Mandans

Fort Clatsop National Memorial
92343 Fort Clatsop Road
Astoria, OR 97103-9197
Demonstrations and talks about Lewis and Clark

Jefferson National Expansion Memorial
11 North Fourth Street
St. Louis, MO 63102
Exhibits on Lewis and Clark; site of their return in 1806.

Lewis and Clark National Historic Trail Interpretive Center
4201 Giant Springs Road
Great Falls, MT 59405-8733
Exhibits about Great Falls portage

Lewis and Clark State Park
21914 Park Loop
Onawa, IA 51040
Copy of boat like the one Lewis and Clark used

Monticello
2 miles (3 kilometers) southeast of Charlottesville, VA 22902
http://www.monticello.org
Thomas Jefferson's home; has display of Lewis and Clark items.

North Dakota Lewis and Clark Interpretive Center/ Fort Mandan
U.S. Highway 83 and North Dakota Highway 200A
Washburn, ND 58577
http://www.fortmandan.org/fortmandan.html
Re-creation of Lewis and Clark's winter quarters

Pompey's Pillar National Monument
25 miles (40 kilometers) east of Billings, Montana
http://www.mt.blm.gov/pillarmon/index.html
Rock formation named for Sacagawea's son

Internet Sites

FactHound offers a safe, fun way to find Internet sites related to this book. All of the sites on FactHound have been researched by our staff.

Here's how:
1. Visit *www.facthound.com*
2. Type in this special code **0736810994** for age-appropriate sites. Or enter a search word related to this book for a more general search.
3. Click on the **Fetch It** button.

FactHound will fetch the best sites for you!

Index